The American People and Nation

D1608727

Michael J. McHugh

Christian Liberty Press
502 W. Euclid Avenue
Arlington Heights, Illinois 60004

This history text was previously entitled *Christian Liberty History Book B.*

Preface

Very few subjects are as important to young people as our nation's Christian heritage. Children in America need to be taught day by day the principles that made our country great.

It is the purpose and goal of *The American People and Nation* to prepare young people to become good citizens. Good citizenship must begin with a study of America's Christian foundations.

Instructors will often need to read parts of this book to their students. Slower readers should be encouraged to participate orally in class discussion until their reading skills mature. A helpful glossary of terms, organized by chapter, is provided at the back of the text and should be referred to on a regular basis. It would be wise for instructors to spend time discussing the pictures, text, and Bible verses with their students.

In addition, students should be encouraged to bring in pictures, flags, or objects that may enhance their history study. Have a variety of books and magazines pertaining to America for the children to read during special class sessions. This type of activity will help broaden the students' interest in history and will also help to enhance their reading skills.

Above all, I sincerely hope that you will be able to encourage your students to develop a genuine interest in American history. May this history study enable you to guide your students to the place where they can understand and appreciate their nation's heritage.

Michael J. McHugh
Arlington Heights, Illinois
1997

"Where the spirit of the Lord is, there is liberty."

II Corinthians 3:17b

THE AMERICAN PEOPLE AND NATION

Contents

Chapter	Page
Preface	
1. An Introduction to History	1 – 5
2. Great Christians of the Past	6 – 14
3. God Uses the Pilgrims to Start a Colony	15 – 18
4. Life in Early America	19 – 24
5. America Unites Into a New Nation	25 – 30
6. Our System of Government	31 – 41
7. A Study of Land and Oceans	42 – 52
8. One Nation Under God	53 – 65
9. America Changes	66 – 74
Glossary	75 – 81
Famous American Songs	82 – 85

1. An Introduction to History

Do you know what the word <u>history</u> means?

History is the story of how God has worked out His plan for men and nations. It is "His story" of man since the beginning of time. History, therefore, must be studied in terms of God's almighty control over the world.

The Holy Bible gives people information on how history began in the book of Genesis.

Copy Genesis 1:1 here. _____

_____

_____

God does everything according to an orderly plan. Nothing in history happens without God's permission. God had an orderly plan when He created the earth and every living thing.

The Bible teaches us that God created man in an orderly way for a special purpose.

1. Copy Genesis 1:27. _____

   _____

2. Who made the earth and every living thing? _____

   _____

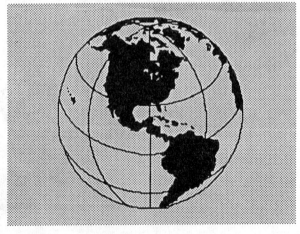

Have you ever asked yourself, "Why did God make the earth?" God made the earth as well as all things in it for His glory.

"For by him were all things created, that are in heaven, and that are in earth... all things were created by him, and for him."
Colossians 1:16

After God formed the earth, He decided that He should create people to live on it. The whole duty of man is to glorify God and keep His commandments. The Bible tells us to:

"Fear God and keep His commandments for this is the whole duty of man."
Ecclesiastes 12:13b

How can boys and girls glorify God in their daily lives?

_____

_____

The Bible, as well as all of history, is filled with stories of great men and women who were used by God to change the world for good.

Can you list the names of three people mentioned in the Bible that lived a life pleasing to God? If so, list the names below:

1. _____ 2. _____ 3. _____

God has a plan for your life. Memorize the Bible verse listed below:

"Trust in the Lord with all thine heart; and lean not unto thine own under- standing. In all thy ways acknowledge Him, and He shall direct thy paths."

Proverbs 3:5, 6

This Bible verse tells us that God has a wonderful plan and purpose for our lives if we look to Him for direction.

Most boys and girls dream of being someone special. Maybe you want to be a mailman or fireman or nurse or missionary. God says that if we love Him, He has greater things for us to do than we can ever dream.

We will study the lives of many people in this book. You will learn that God has used people in very special ways. When you read of how God used these people, think of how He plans to use you. God is preparing you for something special, too.

A wise young person will use his time in school wisely so he is prepared to serve God properly.

In the next chapter we will study the lives of godly people who lived many years ago. This chapter will show us how God helps and blesses people who love and serve Him.

2. Great Christians of the Past

Many years ago, a godly man by the name of John lived on the earth. John was born a few months before baby Jesus was born in Bethlehem. God gave John an important job to do. John was told to make the people ready for Jesus, who would soon begin his public ministry preaching to the people about their sins and calling them to repentance. John became known as "John the Baptist" for he would baptize those people who repented of sin and believed in God. Many people believed the good things that John said concerning Jesus.

The Holy Bible tells us of the life of John the Baptist. We know that John was a righteous servant of God, for the Bible praises John as a faithful man. We can always trust what the Bible says for it is divinely inspired by God.

1. Why did God send John the Baptist into the world?

   _____

2. What nickname did John receive during his travels

   as a preacher of God? _____

3. Why can people trust what the Bible says? _____

   _____

When Jesus visited the earth, a large number of people believed He was the Son of God. However, there were some people who were still blinded by their sins and could not recognize that Jesus was God. One such unbeliever was Saul of Tarsus. Saul refused to believe that Jesus was God.

After Saul became a Christian, God told him to preach the good news of Jesus Christ to everyone who would listen. God also told Saul to change his name to Paul so that people would realize that he was a preacher not only to the Jews, but also to people who were not Jews.

The Holy Bible honors Paul with the title of "apostle." An apostle is someone who received instruction and teaching directly from Jesus Himself. In addition, an apostle was also given special power and authority to teach other people about the things that Jesus told them. The Apostle Paul was directed by God to write a portion of the Bible. We should be very thankful to God for sending this great man of faith into the world!

1. Before the Apostle Paul became a Christian he was

   an _____

2. Paul the Apostle wrote part of the _____.

3. The Holy Bible honors Paul with the title of _____

   _____

4. Jesus told Paul to teach the good news of salvation

   to _____ who would listen.

Draw a picture of your local church in the space below.

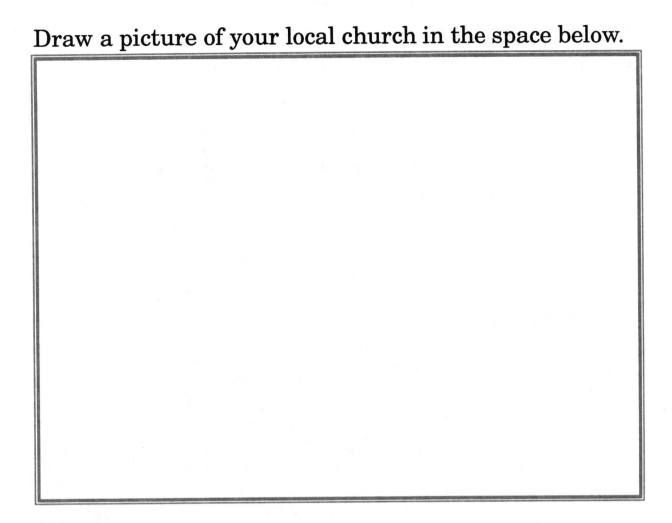

As time passed, people began to explore new lands and travel far distances. In the year 1492, a man named Christopher Columbus decided to sail a ship around the world. Columbus wanted to prove that the world was round instead of flat. Columbus also wanted to discover new lands for the glory of King Jesus.

For many weeks Columbus and his fellow sailors sailed across the wide ocean. Some of the sailors became afraid of the long journey and wanted to go back to their homes. But Columbus was not afraid of being far away from home, for he knew that God would take care of him.

In answer to his prayers, Columbus soon came upon dry land. The new land that Columbus discovered was called America. Columbus and his men landed in America on October 12, 1492.

COLUMBUS AS A BOY

1. Columbus believed that the world was _____.

2. Columbus was a brave man for he knew that _____ would take care of him as he sailed across the ocean.

3. In the year _____ Columbus discovered America.

Color the picture of the sailing ship in the space below.

Several years after Columbus discovered America, God looked down from heaven and saw that many people in the world were still lost in their sins and sad. Even the people who belonged to the church of Jesus Christ had become lazy and confused. So God sent a special person named Martin Luther to the world to turn the hearts of men back to Jesus and the Holy Bible.

Martin Luther lived in a land called Europe. Europe is located many miles away from America. Many years ago people had to sail ships across a very wide ocean to travel from Europe to America. As a matter of fact, Christopher Columbus was one of the first men to sail from the land of Europe to the land we now call America. We should be thankful that God is wise and powerful enough to take care of His people no matter where they live in the world.

Europe

Martin Luther told the people of Europe that they must center their entire lives on the teachings of the Holy Bible. The people of Europe had forgotten that the only way for man to be free from God's righteous anger was through faith in the risen Son of God, Jesus Christ. Thousands of people living in Europe began to change, or "reform," their relationship with God because of the preaching and teaching of Martin Luther. That is why history books tell us that Martin Luther started a "Reformation" in Europe.

Thanks to the efforts of Martin Luther, and by the grace of God, the Christian Church began to grow once again and God's people went forward with new joy and wisdom.

1. God sent a special person named _____ to turn the hearts of men back to Jesus and the Holy Bible.

2. After the "Reformation" in Europe, the Christian Church began to _____ once again.

3. Martin Luther lived in a land called _____.

4. The history books tell us that Martin Luther was used by God to start a _____ in Europe.

A few years after the "Reformation" in Europe, wicked men began to persecute Christian people. They did not like the fact that people lived their lives for the glory of Jesus Christ. God's people were treated with so much hatred and cruelty in Europe that they began to search for a new land where they could worship God freely.

A godly man named William Bradford decided to travel far away from Europe with his Christian friends to find freedom in the land of America. Bradford sailed with other Christians to America on a ship called the *Mayflower*. It was a hard trip, but God brought the tiny ship across the ocean safely. These faithful men and women landed their ship in a place known as Plymouth Rock. These brave Christian travelers became known as "Pilgrims." A Pilgrim is someone who travels from place to place in search of the freedom to worship God.

Color the picture of the *Mayflower* shown below.

William Bradford was elected to be one of the first leaders of the Pilgrims in America. He was a fine leader and governed the people well, for he taught the people how to love God and follow the teachings of the Bible.

We should be very thankful to God for sending William Bradford to guide the Pilgrims in America. In the next chapter we will learn how God used the Pilgrims to start a new nation.

3. God Uses the Pilgrims to Start a Colony

The Pilgrims worked very hard to build a new society that would bring glory to God and advance the Christian Church. Shortly after the Pilgrims landed in America in November 1620, they made an agreement with each other. This agreement was called the "Mayflower Compact" and stated that the Pilgrims would do all that they could to make laws that would enable all people to worship God freely and without persecution. The Pilgrims believed that God created people to live in freedom and not in slavery. We should be thankful for the Pilgrims. They were used by God to set up a truly free society.

Try to memorize the sentence below:

> **"True Christian liberty is not the right to live as we please, but the power to live as God requires."**

The Pilgrims had to work very hard when they first came to America. They had to learn how to plant and harvest food crops. These settlers needed to build a church. They also needed to build homes for their families.

Soon after landing at Plymouth Rock, the Pilgrims met a strange group of people called Indians living in the wilderness. God helped the Pilgrims make friends with the Indians.

The Indians helped the Pilgrims plant corn. A few months later, the Pilgrims had enough food to get them through the cold winter.

To show their love for God, the Pilgrims set aside a special day to give thanks to the Lord. They had a great feast and invited the Indians to share in their joyful gathering. This was the first Thanksgiving Day. Now we celebrate Thanksgiving Day in America every year to show God that we are still thankful for his great blessings.

"Giving thanks always for all things unto God and the Father in the name of our Lord Jesus Christ."

Ephesians 5:20

List three things that you are thankful for:

1. _____ 2. _____ 3. _____

The early American settlers, known as Pilgrims, had very few of the comforts and blessings that we have today. They did not have lots of food. They did not have fancy homes. They did not have many warm clothes to wear or toys to play with. But they were thankful to be in a free land where they could obey God without being persecuted.

3

4

1 2

19

5

18

6

17 7

9 8

16 15

10

14

11

13 12

4. Life in Early America

A few years after the Pilgrim settlers landed in America, more people began to arrive in America by ship. These people came from the land of Europe just like the first group of Pilgrim settlers.

When America was young, there were only small groups of people living in this country. These groups were called colonies. Most of the colonies belonged to a country in Europe named England. England was so far away from the American colonies that it had a hard time trying to control the lives of the colonists. Most of the people who made the difficult voyage from Europe to America came from England. These people wanted to be free from the bad laws that kept them from worshipping God as they believed the Bible required.

1. Small groups of people living together were

   called _____.

2. The American colonies were ruled by a country

   called _____.

3. Most of the early American settlers traveled from Europe to be _____ from bad laws.

The homes in colonial America were plain and made of wooden logs. The homes were often called "log cabins." The homes in early America usually had dirt floors and a huge fireplace. Mothers would cook their family's food in big pots over the fireplace. The fireplace also heated the small log homes during the winter season. Homes long ago did not have electric lights or running water. Families had to use candles to light their homes. Hot and cold water had to be brought into the house in large wooden buckets.

1. In colonial times homes were heated with a _____

_____.

2. Colonial homes did not have electric lights or _____

_____.

Most colonial homes had very little furniture. Fathers often made furniture for their families at home. There were no stores or shops to buy furniture in early America. Children in colonial times often had to sleep with blankets on the floor for they did not have beds! Clothes and blankets were also homemade during colonial times. A special machine known as a "spinning wheel" was used by mothers to make clothes for the family. Little girls often helped their mothers make clothing for other family members.

People in colonial times wore plain clothes. Most of the clothes were homespun. This means that the thread was made on a spinning wheel at home. People used the juice from berries to give clothing color. This process was called dyeing. Clothes were usually just one solid color during this time in history.

True or False:

1. Colonial homes often had very little furniture.

_____

2. Thread for clothing was made on a machine known as a "clothing machine."

_____

3. People long ago used the juice from berries to color their clothing. _____

People who lived during America's colonial period valued education. Most children went to school at home during this time period. Children learned how to read and write from their parents. Parents taught their children to read so they could read the Holy Bible. Most of the great leaders of early American society were home schooled.

Children that went to school outside the home were also taught to read the Bible. The Bible was the first textbook that children read. The Bible also taught children how to obey their parents and others in authority. It is very important for students to obey school rules. Can you write two of the rules you must obey in school in the space below?

1. _____

_____

2. _____

_____

All education is goal oriented. In early America, the goal of education was to teach all there is to know about God and the world He made.

Life was not easy during colonial times. Even young children had to work hard in school and at home. People did find time to relax and play games once in a while. The children played some of the games you play today. They played marbles, leap frog, tag, and ring-around-the-rosy. Older people often played outdoors. They liked to go ice skating, fishing, and hunting. Fishing and hunting were very good games for they helped to put food on the dinner table!

5. America Unites Into a New Nation

The once tiny settlements of the Pilgrims were now growing very large. There were thirteen colonies in America now. Each colony belonged to the country of England. As the colonies grew larger, the King of England made unfair rules for them to obey. The people became very sad and angry. One rule told the settlers they must worship God in the way that the King liked. These rules were making it hard for the settlers to live in freedom.

The King of England wanted to make all the laws or rules for the American colonies. But the people living in the colonies wanted to make their own laws. As time passed by, the people decided they wanted to be free from England's rules.

During this time period, a godly man named Patrick Henry began to encourage the American people to fight against the evil rule of King George III of England.

Patrick Henry

Patrick Henry told the American people that the King of England wanted to rob them of their money and freedom. As time passed by, the people in the colonies began to see that Patrick Henry was right. The King would not let the people live in freedom!

During a large meeting of patriotic colonial leaders, Patrick Henry spoke boldly about the God-given duty of each American to stand up for liberty. Henry said this comment during his speech in 1775:

"Is life so dear, or peace so sweet, as to be purchased at the price of chains and slavery? Forbid it, Almighty God! I know not what course others may take; but as for me, give me liberty, or give me death."

GEORGE WASHINGTON.

In the year 1776, fifty-five brave men met together to decide what to do. They chose George Washington to be their leader. Washington was a very brave man. He led the colonial army into war against England. The army fought England so the colonies could be free.

The leaders of the American colonies wrote a special paper called the Declaration of Independence. They said that the thirteen American colonies did not belong to England anymore. This paper declared that America was now a new nation.

The Declaration of Independence was signed on July 4, 1776. On that day bells rang from all the churches in the land. The people were happy for they now had a new country called the United States of America.

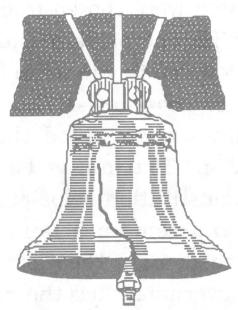
The Liberty Bell

Americans still like to remember that special day. It is our country's birthday. On July 4 we remember how God granted our country freedom. Sometimes we call the fourth day in July Independence Day because it is the day God made us an independent country.

1. The Declaration of _____

    was signed on July 4, 1776.

2. The name of our country is _____

    _____.

By the grace of God, the colonial army won the battle with the army of England. Our new nation was formed into thirteen united states. Our nation needed a new set of laws that were just and fair. We needed laws to protect each person's freedom.

Men were chosen from different parts of our new country to write a new set of laws. These laws were called the Constitution. The Constitution helps our

Betsy Ross making the first flag.

land remain a land of freedom. God gives us our freedoms. The Constitution says that no person or government has the right to take away our freedom.

Our new nation needed a flag in order to identify itself as a separate country. Although no one knows for sure, many people believe that Betsy Ross made the first American flag. The first flag had only thirteen stars for there were only thirteen states when the United States first began.

Color the flag shown below.

Use red to color the lettered stripes. Color around the stars in blue. Leave the rest white.

The flag of the United States is red, white, and blue. There is special meaning for each of the colors in our flag.

Red stands for courage.

White stands for liberty.

Blue stands for loyalty.

Our Flag

The leaders of the original thirteen states also wrote special laws protecting the rights of the people. These laws are called the Bill of Rights. The ten laws that make up the Bill of Rights protect us from cruel and evil leaders. The Bill of Rights guarantees us the right to worship freely. It also says that we have the freedom of speech and movement, freedom to own guns, and freedom to go to church and read the Bible. These laws protect our most basic freedoms. How thankful we should be that we have these freedoms and many more as well!

The thirteen states began to work together and God blessed the United States greatly.

6. Our System of Government

Today a town called Washington, D.C., is the capital of the United States of America. Our leaders meet in Washington, D.C., and make many important decisions. There are three parts to our form of government in America. Below is a picture showing the three basic parts of our government.

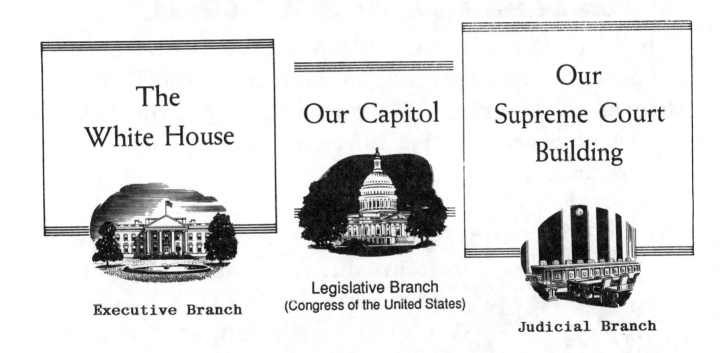

The White House

Executive Branch

Our Capitol

Legislative Branch
(Congress of the United States)

Our Supreme Court Building

Judicial Branch

We will now learn about the White House, the Capitol, and the Supreme Court Building.

The White House is the home of the President of the United States. It is located in our nation's capital city – Washington, D.C.

The President of the United States is the most important person in the government of the United States of America. He makes many important decisions every day that affect the way we live. He leads our country.

George Washington was elected to be the first president of our country in April 1789. He was chosen by the people. He fought for our nation's freedom as general of the army and helped to make our country's laws. George Washington is often called the "Father of our Country." We should be thankful to God for sending us such a good and godly leader.

Since the time George Washington served as president, many great men have served as President of the United States. Americans are able to choose a new president every four years.

Not every girl or boy can grow up to be president, but all boys and girls can do their best to keep America a strong nation under God by learning about its laws and supporting the Constitution. The United States' government was made to be ruled by the people and for the people.

1. The name of the first President of the United States

   is _____.

2. I can help keep America strong by supporting the

   _____ of the United States.

3. The name of the president at this time in our

   nation's history is _____.

4. The president is chosen every _____ years.

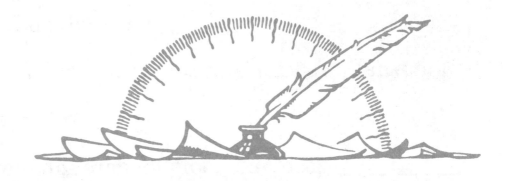

The Capitol

The Capitol building is located in Washington, D.C. This building is very important to our government. It is here that leaders meet from all over the United States. These leaders come together several times each year to make laws for our country.

Each leader that is sent to our nation's Capitol building must first be elected by the people in the area where he lives. The people of the United States have the right to choose who will speak for them in our nation's capital. The people choose new leaders every few years by a process known as "voting." It is important that all patriotic Americans take the time to vote good and Godly leaders into our government.

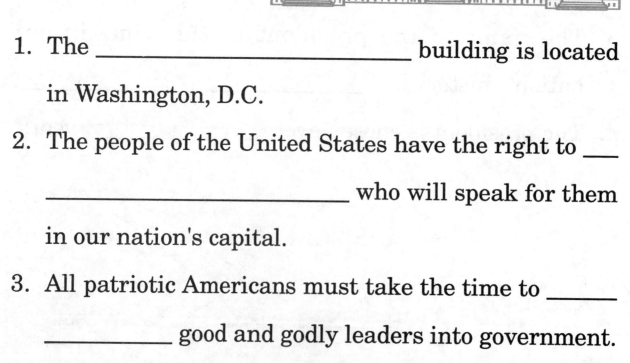

1. The _____ building is located
   in Washington, D.C.

2. The people of the United States have the right to ___
   _____ who will speak for them
   in our nation's capital.

3. All patriotic Americans must take the time to _____
   _____ good and godly leaders into government.

The Supreme Court

Because men are sinners, they often break the laws of God and of men. When people break the law, they must be judged in a court of law. The court must decide if the accused person has done wrong and what the punishment must be if the person is guilty.

God wants all courts to judge people fairly and in harmony with the Holy Bible. God is not pleased with judges who punish people for obeying laws contained in the Bible.

The Supreme Court is the highest court in the United States of America. God wants the Supreme Court to set a godly example for all of the lower courts in America.

The Supreme Court building is located in the city of Washington, D.C. The main purpose of the Supreme Court is to protect all Americans from unjust laws.

Our country is divided into small areas of land called states. Although the United States started with only thirteen states, it soon began to grow larger. Today the United States is made up of fifty states. Have your teacher show you where your state is located on the map. Color your state. Ask your teacher to help you find the United States of America on a globe.

1. The name of the state that I live in is _____

   _____.

2. The name of our country is the _____

   _____ of America.

3. The United States has _____ states.

America is a land richly blessed by God. A minister of God named Samuel Francis Smith wrote the following song in 1832 to thank God for America. Ask your teacher to help you sing this song.

~ AMERICA ~

My country, 'tis of thee
Sweet land of liberty,
    Of thee I sing;
Land where my fathers died
Land of the pilgrim's pride
From every mountain-side
    Let freedom ring.

Let music swell the breeze,
And ring from all the trees
    Sweet freedom's song;
Let mortal tongues awake,
Let all that breathe partake,
Let rocks their silence break –
    The song prolong.

My native country thee,
Land of the noble free,
    Thy name I love;
I love thy rocks and rills,
Thy woods and templed hills;
My heart with rapture thrills
    Like that above.

Our fathers' God, to thee,
Author of liberty,
    To Thee we sing;
Long may our land be bright
With freedom's holy light;
Protect us by Thy might,
    Great God, our King.

Our country's flag has fifty stars. There is one star for each state.

<u>Count the stars on the flag below.</u>

50 United States of America

Ask your teacher if you can see a real American flag. A flag is an important symbol. It lets people know that America is united and free.

When our country was new, there were not as many states in our nation. At first there were only thirteen states. Our country has _____ states today.

The Original Thirteen States

Color each of the thirteen states with a different color.

This is how the United States looked when it was a new country.

The flag of the United States of America is an important symbol. It stands for all that is good and true about America.

All boys and girls should salute the flag and say the pledge to the flag every day in school. When we say the pledge to the flag it is a promise to God that we will honor the country in which He has placed us.

When we say the pledge, we need to stand up straight. We should face the flag. We need to place our right hands on our hearts. God will know by our sincere spirits that we are grateful for the privilege of living in America.

Read and memorize the Pledge of Allegiance shown below. Remember to stand straight and tall when saying it.

I pledge allegiance to the flag
of the United States of America
and to the republic for which it stands
one nation
under God
indivisible
with liberty
and justice for all

The Pledge of Allegiance has many words in it that may be hard for you to understand. Study the words listed below with your teacher and try to understand the pledge better.

1. A <u>pledge</u> is a promise.
2. <u>Allegiance</u> means to be true to something.
3. <u>Republic</u> tells us that America is committed to each person's freedom.
4. <u>Nation</u> means the same thing as country.
5. <u>Indivisible</u> means that it cannot be divided into parts.
6. <u>Liberty</u> means the same thing as freedom.
7. <u>Justice</u> means fairness.

Say the pledge until you understand the meaning.

7. A Study of Land and Oceans

The round planet that we live on is called Earth. In this chapter, we will learn more about the wonderful world that God created. We will see how God placed people and animals on the earth. You will learn about different places and strange things on the earth.

God is always careful to place people in just the right place on earth. God knew when you would be born. He made sure that you were born on just the right place on planet earth.

Remember that God placed you on earth to learn more about Him and the world which He created. Think about how God might use you as you grow up.

Have you ever wondered how the sun works? It is just the right distance away from the earth. God made sure that the sun was just the right distance from the earth so we would not get too hot or too cold. The sun is in the right place to help plants and flowers grow. People could not live on earth if the sun did not work well.

God directs the earth to move around the sun in a circular motion. When the earth has gone around the sun once, an entire year has gone by. God directs the earth to spin like a top each day. Because the earth spins like a top, we have a period of sunshine and darkness each day.

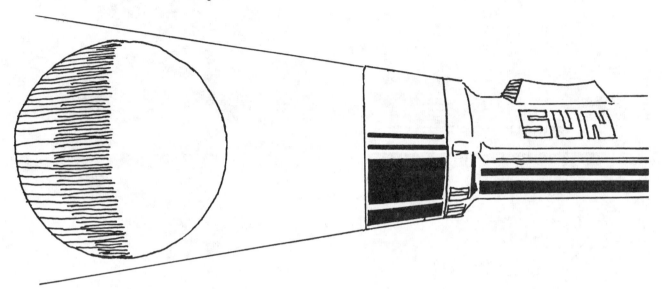

A map is a flat picture of the earth. Can you find the land that you live on in the map pictured below? Color the land that you live on in green.

A globe is a round picture of the earth. It shows us places on the earth. We can learn a lot about our world by studying a globe. Ask your teacher to show you how to use a globe.

1. Atlantic Ocean
2. Pacific Ocean
3. Indian Ocean
4. Arctic Ocean

When God created the earth, He decided to cover most of it with water. The earth has four large areas of water on it called <u>oceans</u>. With your teacher's help, find these four oceans on a globe. Write the names of the oceans in the space below.

1. _____   3. _____

2. _____   4. _____

God also put smaller areas of water on the earth. Small areas of water are often called rivers and lakes. Ask your teacher to show you some rivers and lakes on a globe.

Water is very important to life on earth. If you have ever been thirsty, you know how important water is! People and animals cannot live long without water. This is why the Lord Jesus Christ decided to put so much water on the earth. The picture below shows us how much of the earth is land and how much is water.

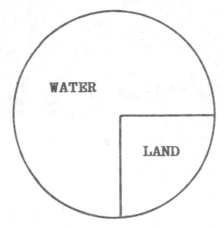

Our wise Creator God makes sure that the earth receives just the right amount of sunshine and water. God uses the sun and the water together to make flowers and plants grow. Thanks to our Heavenly Father's care, the earth brings forth food for our people to eat and stays beautiful with flowers and trees.

List two ways that people use water:

1. _____

2. _____

List two ways that people use the sun:

1. _____

2. _____

"Remember now thy Creator in the days of thy youth."

Ecclesiastes 12:1a

Many years ago when God made the earth, he made seven large areas of land. These large land forms are called <u>continents</u>.

God also made many smaller lands. We call these small land areas <u>islands</u>. An island is a piece of land that is totally surrounded by water. Ask your teacher to show you a picture of an island on a map or globe.

The following map activities will help you to understand where God has placed the seven continents on the earth. Ask your teacher to show you the continents on a map of the world.

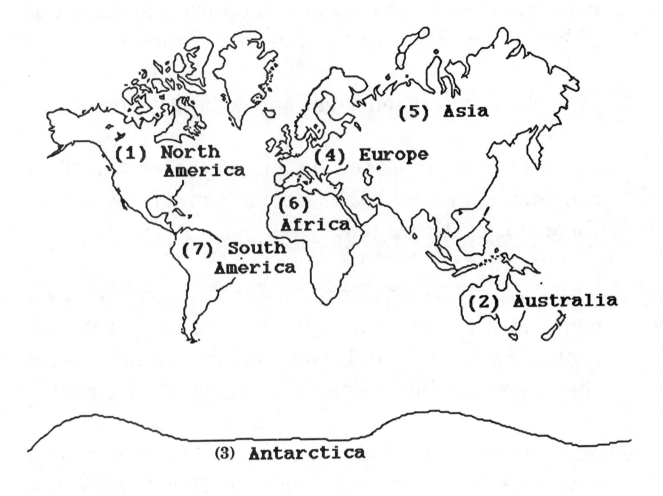

(1) North America
(4) Europe
(5) Asia
(6) Africa
(7) South America
(2) Australia
(3) Antarctica

1. With your teacher's help, locate the seven continents on a world map. Memorize the names of each of the continents. Write the name of each continent in the spaces below.

1. _____ 2. _____

3. _____ 4. _____

5. _____ 6. _____

7. _____

2. Find the continent in which God has placed you to live. Your teacher can help you find the continent of North America. Color this continent orange.

3. Find the smallest continent and color it yellow.

4. One continent is at the bottom of the earth. This continent is so cold that people cannot live on it. Color this continent red.

5. The largest continent on earth is really two continents in one. We divide it because the two continents are very different from each other. Color the larger part blue. Color the smaller part green.

6. You now have only two continents left to discover. One of the continents is called South America because it is located below the continent of North America. Color the continent of South America purple.

7. The last continent for you to locate is called Africa. Africa is located just below the continent of Europe. Ask your teacher to help you locate this continent on the map. Color the continent of Africa brown.

It is interesting to study about where God made man and how people slowly began to spread across the earth.

God made the first man and woman in a beautiful garden called Eden. The garden of Eden was on the continent of Asia.

The first man and woman, Adam and Eve, chose to disobey God. They ate fruit from a tree that God had told them not to touch. The sin of Adam brought a curse upon all mankind. Adam and Eve had to leave the beautiful garden and enter a hard world cursed by sin.

Even though Adam and Eve sinned, God still wanted them to have children and the families of the earth slowly began to grow. For many years, the people that came from Adam and Eve lived near the old garden of Eden. These people also chose to live in sin, so God destroyed them with a world-wide flood. Only a man named Noah and his family were saved in an ark filled with many animals. Noah found grace in God's sight.

As time passed, the people who came after Noah began to fight with each other and to disobey God. The Lord told the people to move away into other parts of the world. Nevertheless, these sinners stayed together and began to build a large tower. While they were building their tower, God decided to change the language that each person spoke. The people became confused because they could not understand each other. A short time later, the people began to move away from each other into different parts of the earth.

The map below shows us how many of these people moved throughout the world. Can you see why the continents of North and South America were among the last to be explored?

Over time, the people of the earth set up small towns in the areas they settled in. These small towns or settlements grew larger with time and often created a nation. A nation is a large group of people who live in the same land and share the same leaders or laws.

When God created many different languages, He knew that people would move far away and start their own countries. Even today, the people and nations of the earth often stay apart because they speak different languages. In this way, no one group of sinners can become too powerful and take over the whole earth. Do you now understand how God made the nations and why people speak different languages?

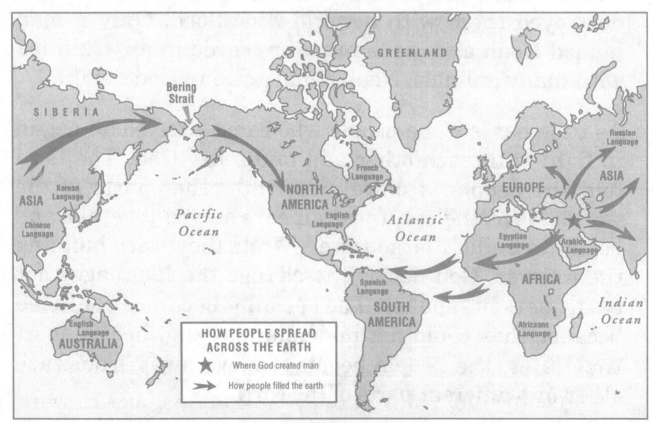

The United States of America

This is a map of North America. Find the areas that belong to the United States. Color just the land areas of the United States. We live in the United States of America. Sometimes our country is simply called America.

God has made America a special land. America is special because people are free to choose where they wish to work. People can also choose where they will live. The people of America can choose their leaders. Parents in America are free to educate their own children.

America is special because in many of the countries of the world, there is no freedom. In much of the world today, it is a crime to tell others about Jesus and the Bible. In America, however, we do not need to fear evil men. God has truly blessed the people of America for they can serve and worship God freely.

We should be very thankful for the many freedoms that we have in America. We should also remember to work and pray for people living in other parts of the world that are not free to serve God.

"Remember those that are in bonds, as bound with them..."

Hebrews 13:3a

Copy this Bible verse here. _____

_____

_____

All of the countries of the world belong to God. He created them out of nothing. It is God's wisdom and power that keeps the world together. Someday in the future, God's Son, Jesus Christ, will come and visit our world again. He will judge the countries and people of the world as the Almighty King. Only those people who love and serve King Jesus on earth will be able to go to a new land called Heaven. After Jesus decides who will go to Heaven with Him, He will destroy the earth completely. Then all of God's people will live together in a great new land. How happy we should be to know that God's blessings in this life will be even better when we reach our home in Heaven.

Come unto me, all ye that labour and are heavy laden and I will give you rest.
Matthew 11:28

8. One Nation Under God

As America continued to grow, so did its problems. Many people felt that the government was growing faster than the nation. People that lived in the southern or lower states did not like the federal government taking away their power. The United States' Constitution promised that all states would be able to keep the power to manage their own citizens.

The people that lived in the lower or southern part of the United States became so upset that they decided to leave and start their own nation. The people in the upper or northern part of the United States decided to fight a war with the people in the south. Our country became divided by a civil war.

Many good men and women on both sides were hurt or killed. After a few years of fighting, the people in the south decided to give up fighting. America became a united nation again because the war was over.

God helped the people of the United States to see their stubbornness and pride. After the war was over, God also helped the people of America become friends again.

1. The people of the northern states decided to fight a

   _____ war with the people of the

   southern states.

2. After the war was over, God also helped the people

   of America to become _____ again.

America has changed over the years. When America was still quite young, people used to travel slowly from place to place. Early travelers were usually called pioneers. They often traveled by  riding horses. Horses also helped to pull wagons and carts for the early American pioneers.

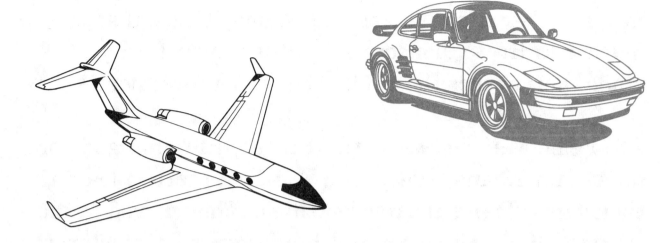

We have many kinds of transportation today. Transportation has changed our nation. For example, we now travel from place to place in cars and planes, not horses and wagons.

1. Can you name some other ways we travel today? ___

   _____

   _____

2. Cars, planes, and engine powered ships help man to move much faster than he did years ago. How did faster travel help America grow larger? _____

   _____

   _____

In addition to transportation, machines also helped America to grow.

Pioneers in early America lived for the most part on farms. They made almost all of the things that they needed to live. Pioneers grew their own food. They made their own clothes. They built their own homes.

After the War Between the States, life changed for many Americans. People in America started leaving their farms to live in crowded cities. They moved to the cities to find work. Special buildings called factories were built so that people could now make more things faster. People could now sell more of the things that they made. This helped America to grow.

After the American people started to make more things, they invented special tools and machines to help them work. Many factory buildings were filled with special tools like electric saws and sewing machines so people could make things faster. Tools and machines are very important. They help us work neatly and quickly.

Can you name some of the tools that you have around

your home? _____

_____

God expects us to work hard. America is a great nation that owns many nice things because its people work hard. Copy this Bible verse in the space below.

"Whatsoever thy hand findeth to do, do it with thy might;"

Ecclesiastes 9:10a

The year 1900 began a new century for the United States of America and for the world. America was fast becoming a powerful nation because it could produce more products than any other country. The American people invented many wonderful products during this time in its history. America gave the world radios, automobiles, televisions, telephones, record players, airplanes, and large ships.

In addition to material products, America gave the world spiritual leadership and brotherly love. Christian missionaries visited many poor and needy countries in distant lands. These concerned Americans brought much needed food to hungry people. In addition to food and clothing, American missionaries brought the life giving message that Jesus Christ is the savior of the world. The American people were not selfish. Rather, they shared the good things that they had with others in the world.

In the year 1914, a war started on the continent of Europe. Since many Americans came from Europe, they were concerned about this war and how some of their old friends would survive the fighting. The war dragged on three long years and became so big that it seemed as though the whole world was at war. This is why this war in Europe is known as the First World War. Finally in 1917, the United States became involved in World War I and sent soldiers to help the countries in Europe that it liked. America helped the nations of France, Great Britain, and Belgium put an end to the war in Europe.

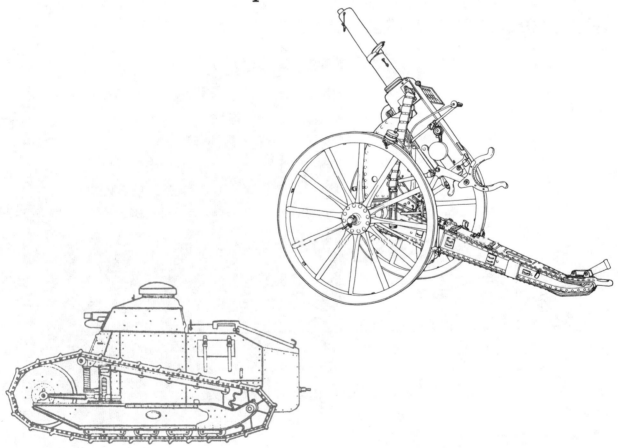

The world was again grateful to the United States for helping to put an end to a very terrible war.

A few years after World War I, a young man by the name of Charles Lindbergh made history. Lindbergh was the first person to fly an airplane from the United States to Europe. This wonderful event opened up a new era in world travel. Lindbergh showed the people of the world that an airplane could permit people to travel around the world faster than ever before. Have you ever flown in an airplane?

The name of the airplane used by Lindbergh in 1927 was the *Spirit of St. Louis*.

<u>Color the airplane shown below.</u>

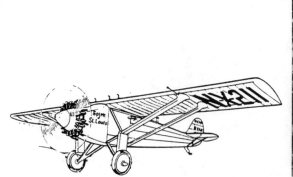

The *Spirit of St. Louis* is now hanging in a large museum called the Smithsonian Institute located in Washington, D.C.

In October 1929, our nation was humbled by God with money problems. America had disobeyed God's law about how money should be used. Many people in America were spending money that they had not earned yet. People were borrowing large sums of money from banks to buy things that they wanted instead of waiting patiently for the Lord to provide. America's money problems lasted several years and caused many people in America to lose everything they once owned. This time period is now known as the "Great Depression."

Sadly, although God delivered America from her money crisis, many people still refused to reform their poor use of money. The youth of America can help to lead America back to following God's laws for money by staying out of debt. Here are some important rules for the use of money:

1. Only borrow money if it is an emergency.
2. Always pay back money that you borrowed as fast as possible.
3. Do not borrow money from more than one person at the same time.
4. Never borrow money from people who make you pay back more money than you borrowed.

In the year 1941, a nation called Japan sent airplanes to a place called Hawaii and dropped bombs on American soldiers. This very bad act forced the United States to declare war against Japan. Many countries around the world were also fighting with each other at this time. There was so much fighting around the world at this time that this war became known as World War II. Many people were hurt or killed during this big war. Some people in America believed that America should stay out of the war and let the world take care of itself. However, this thinking was not true to the spirit that made America free. So the American people decided to fight against those people in the world that wanted to make people into slaves.

The American people believed that it was their duty to stand up for and defend freedom and liberty.

Memorize the sentence listed below:

> "God grants liberty only to those who love it, and are always ready to fight for it."
> Daniel Webster

During this time of world war, the United States government chose an army general named Douglas MacArthur to lead the fight against Japan. General MacArthur was a brave and noble leader. He trusted that Almighty God would grant the American soldiers victory as they fought the Japanese soldiers.

After years of hard fighting on both sides, the Lord began to answer the prayers of General Douglas MacArthur. The soldiers of Japan were forced to give up more and more of the land that they had stolen from other nations in the Far East. The freedom-loving people of the world were encouraged as they began to see the evil dictators in Japan losing power.

By God's grace, World War II finally ended on August 14, 1945. The nation of Japan stopped fighting with the United States and our soldiers helped to teach the people of Japan how to be peace loving. Today, the people of Japan have become friends with the people of the United States.

Since the time of World War II, the United States has continued to help nations around the world that are under attack by evil forces. A powerful and evil system of government called Communism has started many wars in recent years. In addition, some of the people who follow the ideas of Communism have killed millions of people who love God and believe in freedom. Every person who lives in freedom should pray and work so that Communism will be stopped.

America's fortieth president, Ronald Reagan, told the truth when he said that Communism was an evil system. A man of God by the name of Rev. Levi Wisner said this about freedom:

"He who will not use his freedom to preserve his freedom does not deserve his freedom."

It is the duty of every American, young or old, to stand up for the fact that God created all people to live in freedom.

General Douglas MacArthur

The people of the United States have always been proud of the fact that God has made them free. As you may recall, America became a free nation in the year 1776. In 1776 the Declaration of Independence was signed. This paper said that America was now free from the control of other nations or people.

A large bell was rung in 1776 to show how happy we were to be a free nation. This large bell weighs 2,000 pounds and is known as the Liberty Bell. Our nation's Liberty Bell was cracked very badly many years ago. Although the bell is no longer rung, it still stands as an important symbol of liberty.

<u>Color the picture of the Liberty Bell below.</u>

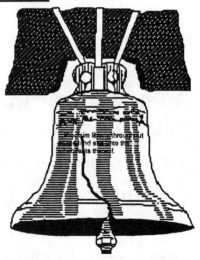

Our Liberty Bell has a Bible verse printed on its face. Ask your teacher to help you memorize this Bible verse.

"...Proclaim liberty throughout all the land unto all the inhabitants thereof."

Leviticus 25:10

9. America Changes

Our nation continued to grow and change. Some of the changes were good, and some were bad.

Many people in America today have forgotten God. They worship and praise man-made things. They do not care to thank God for His blessings. They forget that God made the earth and owns everything in it. This foolish way of thinking is very bad. We must honor God above all earthly things. We must encourage other people in America to turn their minds and hearts to God.

In America today we see many new inventions. These inventions continue to cause America to change. Tractors that run by engine help farmers in the field. Telephones help us to talk to people who live far away. Washers and dryers help mothers at home. Computers help make work easier at the office. Can you name two other modern inventions that you use every day? List them in the space below.

1. _____

2. _____

America's cities have changed. Modern cities have very tall buildings called skyscrapers. Have you ever seen a skyscraper?

A wonderful event took place in the year 1969. During that year, our nation landed a spaceship on the moon. For the first time in history, a man was able to walk on the moon. The American people were excited as they watched their TV sets and saw astronauts place a U.S. flag on the moon.

Since the late 1960s, the United States has continued to explore outer space. President George Bush told the American people in 1990 that our nation would try to land a spaceship on the planet Mars after a few years.

<u>Color the picture of the spaceship</u>

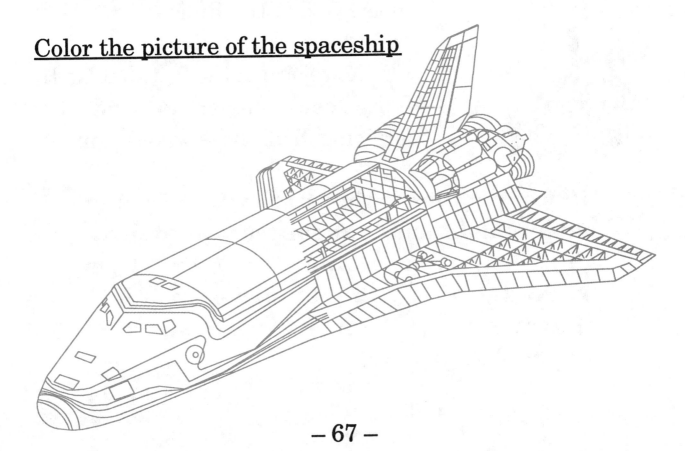

The way that Americans travel keeps changing as well. Airplanes take people around the world in just a few hours. Spaceships take men to the moon. Some cars today are made out of plastic and are powered by electricity.

Over the years, America has even changed its money. Our coins now have our nation's motto printed on them. A motto is a short statement. Our country's motto is "In God We Trust." Ask your teacher to show you where this motto is printed on our money.

We must be very careful as Christians not to trust in money. Sadly, many people in America have forgotten to place their trust in the God of the Bible.

We can rejoice in the fact that God's Son, Jesus Christ, is kind and forgiving to all those who repent.

"If my people, which are called by my name, shall humble themselves, and pray, and seek my face, and turn from their wicked ways; then I will hear from heaven, and will forgive their sin, and will heal their land."

II Chronicles 7:14

1. Our nation's motto is, "In _____ We Trust."

2. Over the years, America has even changed its

The Statue of Liberty stands on an island near the city of New York. It was given to the United States by the people of France. They wanted to help us celebrate our country's 100th birthday.

The Statue of Liberty is the largest statue ever made. It is over 300 feet from sea level to the tip of its torch. That is the length of one football field. The torch at the top is so large that it can hold twelve people.

A well known poem is written at the base of the statue. It lets the world know how Americans feel towards the people of the world. It says, "Give me your tired, your poor ..."

Many poor and needy people come to America from other lands. Thousands of people that have come to

America have passed the Statue of Liberty. The statue reminds them of what America offers the world — liberty and justice for all. Color the torch yellow and the statue green.

Keeping America Beautiful

God has blessed us with a beautiful land. He has given us a land of clear lakes and pretty flowers; a land of beautiful animals and lovely parks.

God told Adam and Eve to take care of the earth. We should take care of everything we have. We should not be messy or wasteful. God wants us to keep our homes, our neighborhoods, and our parks neat and clean. If we will be faithful in the task of keeping America beautiful, then others can enjoy America, too!

"Let all things be done decently and in order."

I Corinthians 14:40

Copy the Bible verse here. _____

_____

_____

As soon as God created man, he gave him this command:

> "Be fruitful, and multiply, and replenish the earth, and subdue it: and have dominion over...every living thing upon the earth."

Genesis 1:28

From the beginning of the world, God had given man the responsibility to properly take care of the world God created. This means that each person has the God-given duty to use the things of this world in a responsible way.

List two things that you can do to help bring back the beauty of God's creation in your own home or city.

1. _____

_____

2. _____

_____

RECYCLING

You have studied many things about the history of the world and our nation. You have learned that God created the world. You have also learned that God decides what changes will happen in the world He has created.

Although time changes all things on earth, it does not change God. Time does not change God for God is unchangeable. God is above time. This is important to remember because God wants us to know that He will be with us at all times. God guides us each day as we pray to Him for help.

In the Bible we read:

"To everything there is a season, and a time to every purpose under the heaven:"

Ecclesiastes 3:1

Have you ever wondered why you were born? The Bible teaches us that God created all people to love and serve Him. God has a special plan for your life. He wants you to look to him for guidance.

God's Word says:

> "Trust in the Lord with all thine heart; and lean not unto thine own understanding. In all thy ways acknowledge Him, and He shall direct thy paths."
>
> Proverbs 3:5,6

Never forget that this world is under God's control. He took great care to make each thing in a special way for your enjoyment. Worship the great Creator, my young friends. God is the key to true wisdom and happiness.

~ GOD BLESS AMERICA* ~

God bless America!
Land that I love,
Stand beside her and guide her
Through the night with a light from above.
From the mountains to the prairies,
To the ocean white with foam,
God bless America, my home sweet home,
God bless America, my home sweet home.

* *God Bless America*, by Irving Berlin, copyright 1939, Herbert Bayard Swope, Theodore Roosevelt, Jr., and Gene Tunney , as Trustees. Used by permission of Irving Berlin Music Corporation.

Glossary

<u>Words to know from chapter one:</u>

Acknowledge   to pay attention to someone or something

Almighty   all powerful – more powerful than anything on earth

Change   to make something different than it once was

Commandments   direct orders from someone in authority

Create   to make something new out of nothing

Duty   obligation or responsibility

Earth   the world in which we live

Genesis   the name given to the first book in the Bible

Orderly   having a neat appearance

Mentioned   to talk about something

Missionary   a person who travels to different parts of the world to tell people about God

Preparing   making something ready to use

Study   to think about something in a detailed way

Wisely   doing something God's way

Words to know from chapter two:

Ascended	going in an upward direction
Blinded	when a person loses the ability to see things
Discover	to find something
Europe	one of the seven continents
Faith	believing in something you can not see or feel
Inspired	a person who is under God's direct influence
Jesus	the only person that is perfectly man and perfectly God
Judea	a small country located far away from America
Obedience	doing what you are told to do
Persecuted	when people are treated badly and unfairly
Preaching	telling groups of people about God
Reform	to make something better
Repentance	the act of turning away from evil
Righteous	pure and holy according to the Bible
Traveled	moving from one place to another
Wicked	evil

Words to know from chapter three:

Agreement	when people decide to think the same way
Blessings	good things that come from God
Celebrate	to remember something in a special way
Joyful	happy
Slavery	being under the total control of another
Wilderness	natural forest area that has not been settled by man
Worship	to show great respect and honor to someone or something

Words to know from chapter four:

Difficult	hard
Furniture	things that people use for living in a house, such as beds, chairs, and tables
Hunting	searching after something to capture it
Plain	simple – not fancy
Society	people living together as a group
Voyage	the travel of a ship across water from place to place

Words to know from chapter five:

Army   an organized group of people who fight for a cause

Constitution   the most important rules of a nation

Declaration   to say something openly before the people

Grace   getting something we don't deserve

Guarantee   to promise or assure

Identify   to make something known

Independent   operating without the support of others

King   a powerful person who rules over a group of people

Liberty   the power to do what God requires people to do on earth

Patriot   a person who supports the just interests of his country

Protect   to keep something from harm

Words to know from chapter six:

Globe   a three dimensional model of the earth

Grateful   to feel very thankful for something received

Judges   the people who decide whether certain things on earth are right or wrong and punish evil

Sincere   honest and true

Wrong   any disobedience to God's Word

Words to know from chapter seven:

Beauty   something that is pretty

Born   brought to life

Heaven   God's home up in the sky

Nature   the things that God created so people could live on earth (plants, trees, animals)

Nothing   empty

Spin   to turn completely around

Surrounded   covered on all sides

Thirsty   in need of something to drink

Visit   to go somewhere for a time

Words to know from chapter eight:

Crowded   a place that is full of things or people

Farm   a place where people raise animals and grow food

Federal   central

Leave   to travel away from something

Pioneers   people who travel to new parts of the earth

Pride   an overly high belief in yourself instead of in God

Transportation   the process of going from place to place

Words to know from chapter nine:

Acknowledge   to admit or confess that something is true

Creator   one of the names given to God

Electricity   the power that makes lights and machines work

France   a country on the continent of Europe

Invention   something that is made for the first time

Money   a name given to valuable coins and paper put out by the government

Unchangeable   always able to stay the same

Wasteful   failing to make good use of something

Worship   the act of showing great love or devotion for someone or something

Famous American Songs

The song Dixie has become a favorite of many Americans. Ask your teacher to help you sing this song.

~ DIXIE* ~

I wish I was in the land of cotton,
Old times there are not forgotten;
Look away, look away, look away, Dixie land!
In Dixie land where I was born in,
Early on one frosty mornin',
Look away, look away, look away, Dixie Land!

(*Chorus*)
Then I wish I was in Dixie! Hooray! Hooray!
In Dixie land we'll take our stand,
to live and die in Dixie,
Away, away, away down south in Dixie!

This world was made in just six days,
And finished up in various ways.
Look away! look away! look away! Dixie land!
They then made Dixie trim and nice,
And Adam called it "Paradise."
Look away! look away! look away! Dixie land!

(Chorus)

There's buckwheat cakes and Injun batter,
Makes you fat or a little fatter;
Look away, look away, look away, Dixie land!
Then hoe it down and scratch your gravel,
To Dixie's land I'm bound to travel;
Look away, look away, look away, Dixie land!

(Chorus)

* The words of this song were written by Daniel D. Emmett.

Honor the LORD from your wealth, and from the first of all your produce; so your barns will be filled with plenty, and your vats will overflow with new wine (Proverbs 3:9, 10).

Famous American Songs

This song tells us of America's true source of strength – faith and trust in God. Ask your teacher to help you sing this song.

~AMERICA THE BEAUTIFUL* ~

O beautiful for spacious skies,
For amber waves of grain,
For purple mountain majesties
Above the fruited plain!
America! America!
God shed His grace on thee
And crown thy good with brotherhood
From sea to shining sea!

O beautiful for pilgrim feet,
Whose stern, impassioned stress
A thoroughfare for freedom beat
Across the wilderness!
America! America!
God mend thine every flaw,
Confirm thy soul in self-control,
Thy liberty in law!

O beautiful for heroes proved
In liberating strife,
Who more than self their country loved,
And mercy more than life!
America! America!
May God thy gold refine
Till all success be nobleness
And every gain divine!

O beautiful for patriot dream
That sees beyond the years
Thine alabaster cities gleam
Undimmed by human tears!
America! America!
God shed His grace on thee
And crown thy good with brotherhood
From sea to shining sea!

* This song was written by Katherine Lee Bates.

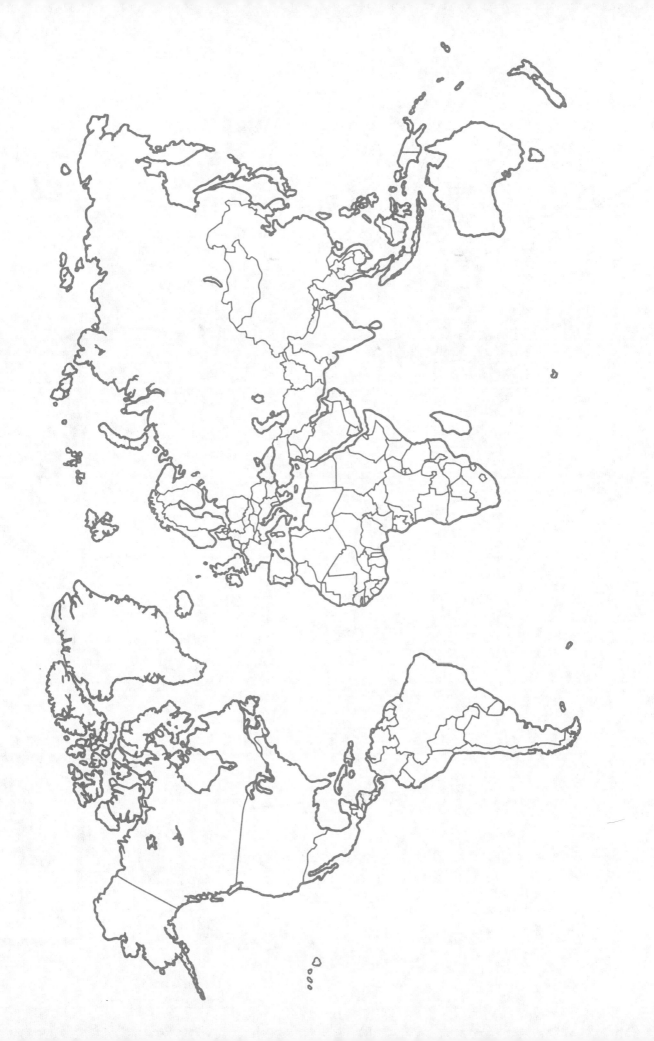